Curating the House of Nostalgia

Cover art: Cara Murray, *What's Left Behind*, Gouache on canvas

ISBN: 9781732940697
Library of Congress Control Number: 2020938048

Published by Sheila-Na-Gig Editions
Russell, KY
www.sheilanagigblog.com

*To those spirit-sustainable, wild northern havens of fireweed,
mountain shadow, and wind.*

***

To Rie: Be perennial in your joy and hopefulness.

***

In memory of my compass-bearer Bruce – Always

Curating the House of Nostalgia

poems

Kersten Christianson

Sheila-Na-Gig Editions
Volume 6

Gratitude

Thank you to the Dyea Bradys (Jeff, Dorothy, and Annie) for their sharing of the Mary Jane cabin and forested space during my summer 2018 writing residency with Alderworks Alaska Writers & Artists Retreat. Thank you for offering me this place to put words in order and find a healing path.

I am further grateful to the Alaska Statewide Poetry Contest for placing "The Ungulate's Jaw," "Katie's Cabin," "Curios," and "Curate."

Heartfelt gratitude to my fellow editors, volunteers, and Alaska women writers at *Alaska Women Speak*, as well as Blue Canoe writers, along with my peers and professors through the University of Alaska Low-Residency MFA program. You have all been a source of inspiration, good ear, and offered sweet friendship throughout the years.

Thank you to artist Cara Jane Murray for recreating *What's Left Behind* for cover placement. Special appreciation to poets Vivian Faith Prescott, Caroline Goodwin, and Carol Birrell for giving this collection a read and an endorsement, and to Sheila-Na-Gig Editions editor, Hayley Mitchell Haugen, for moving this collection into the reading world.

To friends and family who have had my back these last few staggering years — I dare not mention you by name, in case I inadvertently leave someone out. You have gifted me peace of mind and reunion with wildness. Thank you for blank books, *caw-caw*ing at ravens, all-night dancing, gin & tonics, online Scrabbling, doorknob installing, garage emptying, tarot card reading, camping out, random texting, hitting the road, forget-me-not beading, Solstice celebrating, daughter cake baking, salmon-sharing, Bruce storytelling, shenanigans and crimes, Justin Trudeau hand-shaking, check-ins, last minute proofreading, and dearest greetings of well-being, hope, and resilience. My gratitude does not cover all I owe you in return.

Acknowledgments

Allegro Poetry: "Road Trip" retitled "Cassiar"

Ariel Chart: "Harvest Moon Aubade"

Ascent: "Tsunami"

Between These Shores Literary & Arts Annual: "Bohemian"

Cherry House Press: "Little Salmon Lake"

Cirque Journal: "Stjerne," "The Superstition Mountains"

Dream Tiger Press: "96% of the universe," "Moonset"

Foxglove Journal: "Da Eye Wifey / Woods Number 1"

Fredericksburg Literary & Art Review: "Serendipitous," "The Ungulate's Jaw"

Gold Dust Poetry: "Assemblage"

Hedge Apple: "Signs"

Ink Drift: "Dutch Fry Baby"

Kallisto Gaia: "Keno Hill"

Ketchikan Writes Literary Zine 2: "Island of Lost"

Little Dog Poetry: "Diminishing Wind"

Minerva Rising: "Kluane Lake"

Moledro Magazine: "Sometimes"

Moria: "Charged Particles"

Not Your Mother's Breast Milk: "Used Goods"

Peatsmoke Journal: "Prayer for the Wildness"

Peeking Cat Poetry: "Minus Tide"

Picaroon Poetry: "Cèilidh for Angus"

Porkbelly Press/Sugared Water: "Katie's Cabin"

San Pedro River Review: "Honey Sound," "Quartz"

Sheila-Na-Gig Online: "Le Creuset," "Stjerne," "The Geography of Grief," "To the Bare Salmonberry Branch in Winter Cold," "You Choose Your Solitude"

Silkworm: "Curate"

Slipstream: "Curate"

Sooth Swarm Journal: "Beyond Neptune"

The Bangor Literary Journal: "96% of the universe"

The Borfski Press: "Status Update"

The Fredericksburg Literary & Art Review: "The Ungulate's Jaw"

The Local Train Mag: "All Good Things Gray"

The Northern Review: "Crop"

The Poetry Shed: "Curios"

Tidal Echoes: "Of Alderaan"

Trailer Park Quarterly: "Used Goods"

What Caught Raven's Eye: "Silver Trail, Yukon," "Sometimes"

Whiskey Island: "Men Who Serve You Coffee"

Wild Musette: "Cèilidh for Angus"

Wildhood: "Heartwood"

Willow Lit: "Second-Hand"

World Enough Writers: "Dutch Fry Baby"

13 Chairs: "Silver Trail, Yukon"

Contents

Mountain

Clutter

Cataclysm

Astral

Juncture

Epilogue

"i carry your heart (i carry it in my heart)"

--e.e. cummings

Mountain

Curate

In the shadow of the Kluane squats the House of Nostalgia, its portals shuttered with plywood eyelids, tangled weeds its lashes: Hooker's Oat Grass, Sedge, Foxtail. I have heard it hoards toy trains standing still, hockey pucks without a match, driftwood shaped like an unruly midwife birthing long-silenced boat motors, salt air-crusted license plates: Yukon, Alaska, Germany. From a high shelf watches the gossamer skull of a horse recovered from the Dalton Trail, its halves stitched whole with the hair of a wild Russian boar. Shadows of meteoric leaves, slivers of sun flicker-jig in the wind, slink through the cracks to burnish cobwebs, dust, errant cottonwood seeds drifting from head to heart. This could be the home of the 50,000-year-old wolf pup gleaned from permafrost near Dawson City by a miner toiling under high summer sun, her skin a tight drum measuring the back-handed beating of time, her lashes a reluctant wonder along her cheek. Slivers of sun ignite darkness, spotlight the minions that parade my own needled nostalgia, the past a violet-green swallow at midnight in June. In winter, I once held tightly another's hand here whispering, *Listen. Listen to the absence of sound, the sound of stars. We belong here.*

Buddha says something
like this: Love much, live gently,
know when to let go.

Keno Hill

A summit sign
posts cities, distances
in kilometers, dim
bearing on the lodge-
pole pine rooted
at km 6.

Our pitted road
footnotes clusters of wild
rhubarb, willow, white
mountain heather,
a butterfly trail.

My zenith,
with you I bask,
trek off the chart.
Skin to skin,
we love our way
through a bonfire
north.

Katie's Cabin

I.

There
one day – teacup
in the sink, sewing machine propped
in an upstairs window, worn
jacket tatters in an open
closet, half-empty bottle
of Vodka, car keys,
mummified cat – gone
the next.

II.

House locked tightly, window
views screened, haphazard
blinds. Sun kindles her prisms
suspended in time by fishing line thumb-
tacked to the ceiling, blazes light
in the peaks and valleys of once-found stones –
rose and purple quartz – gathered by hand,
collected in an earthen pot
on a windowsill.

III.

We've not met,
but I picture her facing a sun-
warmed window. Her dust devil
memories spiraling in dry city streets,
her legs tucked in by a crocheted blanket.
Her sons will sell her 30-year home
in the Kluane.

IV.

Mice have moved in. They whisk
across countertops, through the walls,
nest in couch cushions. Green-
house, smoker, mosquito-
meshed gazebo. Doors perch single-
hinged against jambs, wait for a warm-
palmed open
and close.

V.

In the yard, weeds knot the garden,
rhubarb skirts the western edge,
reaches for high slopes and day-
light. Arctic poppies hop-
scotch a path to the Volkswagen
bug tangled in a stand of birch.
Missing two wheels,
all windows, I plot
the perfect bed
of nasturtia.

VI.

I'll knock at her door,
but there won't be an answer,
no call to come in. I'll walk
the perimeters of her land, skim
my fingertips along the blades
of waist-high grass, past the bed
of a moose, into the bright-
sunned sky.

The Superstition Mountains

-For the artist Ettore "Ted" DeGrazia.

My long-dead grandmother
came to me in a dream.
A traveler in this world,

she took my hand and led me
along a weaver's needle path
into the eye of a rocky range.

A petulant child, the wind kicked
at the dust of the desert trail long-
traveled by black bear.

At the crown, the artist, his bonfire.
With sly grin, he hurled his art:
sunshine children, gaunt fox,

winged and haloed women, tired
horse, leaping pony, flowers
and stars, mother and child.

His creations fed the maw
of oiled flames, carried
the acrylic hues of amber,

of titian, of perse to charred
skies. My grandmother's hand,
her touch, the flicker of a candle.

Kluane Lake

Oddly windless, a still cup of cooled tea.
A lone loon pens the water's only wake,

the toppled script across a blank page,
cries a language my heart translates

only in verbs: Stay. Begin. Live.
Later, at the border of sleep

and wakefulness, the winds return
home, retune the lake's song.

Cassiar

When driving
the Alaska Highway
it is reliable advice

to don a watch;
tundra, taiga,
boreal forest

won't carry a Wi-Fi
signal and anyway,
your smartphone's

battery will wither
after 2 1/2 days
driving wilderness

roads. And really
it won't matter;
your eyes now scan

for black bears
grazing dandelions,
she-fox carrying

her kit alongside
a remote stretch
of trenched blacktop.

Jade in the mountains,
in the lakes, named
and not. You imagine

humdrum internet still
2 days out, scrolling
updates at Tim Horton's

over a Double-Double
and a box of Timbits,
but this won't matter,

really; your mind
blown, like strips
of tire in the shoulder,

still hazed by wind
and solitude.

Silver Trail, Yukon

After the 8-minute wait for a green light
(the sole streetlight north of Whitehorse),
on the barren Stewart Crossing Bridge
citing construction and no traffic
in any direction, we nosed our way
northeast from firm, compacted road

to washboard gravel, to dirt, to mud
to occasional sinkhole. This narrowing
road chases the Silver Trail, its cyclical
bust boom. 125 miners laid off Wednesday:
Drop of silver, empty mines, and pockets.
But the new grocery store recently opened

in Mayo, the town whose library and liquor
store share space, and it's moose season.
The latest international adventurer
misplaced in the wild was located
after a three-day search. In Keno, Mike
and his girl return with enough greens,

olives, and feta to mix Greek salad
for the community supper. They'll serve
all 20 tonight, the old men with accents, those
who stumble in from cabins made crooked
by the joust between permafrost and heat. Cross-
eyed and gentle, a stray dog nuzzles our hands.

How did he find his way down this fragmentary
road? Fireweed bloom, blazed pomegranate
to the pinnacle of its stalk, casts its pungent
honey sweet magic into the warm winds
of summer, to the apocalyptic clouds
congregating along the ridge.

You Choose Your Solitude

It's easy to live with nothing.

The kitchen without a table
the phone number
nobody calls.

Is it so easy?

In Klukshu the snow
curls and gathers,
blankets a far-flung
highway.

Is it so easy?

Yes. Cleave
your world in two,
the halves of a honeydew
made whole. Your scrawled
name in the snow.

The Book of Ursula

Cosmic mother,
poetry by flame,
you walk in a boreal

of words.
Because your eyes
adjust to dim light

you follow a path
to the far riverbank,
trail the wake

of folded paper
boats ablaze
with tiny lanterns.

In the distance,
a tinny bell in the wind.
You have arrived.

Leaving Omelas

We, too, will turn
our backs to the crème
brûléed crust of self-
proclaimed greatness,

of sea-breezed communion,
plastic flowers, copulations

along the shore.
We will bid riddance
to tambourine temples,
wind-snapped banners.

We will lift the child
from concrete

and cage, offer
water, sweet fruit,
clean clothing.
We will carry

this child from shadow
to the light

of a reunited family.
Only then can we return
to the mountain knowing
we tried.

"The Ones Who Walk Away from Omelas," Ursula K. Le Guin, 1973

From Night's Window

Bee balm & forget-me-nots,
lupine cluster bomb
by north's long sun

Thin, white cuticle
of shape shifting moon
won't be viewed

from this June mountain
of birch trees & burls
crinkled vellum, pregnant

belly knotted wood. Pack
your magic & drive; wander
widely the pockmarked road.

Find the place where you think
you can translate the wind,
the silence, into wild.

Serendipitous

That sear of lemonade-sipping
sun, sapsucker skittering talons
across the wood porch, eyeballing
through your open-hearted door.

A windchime from home (stringed
spoons, beads) chants a Taiya rivershed
song. You scribe under a blanket fort
mountain to the cadenced flap shuffle

of cottonwood leaves. The matriarchal
wolf dog visits twice a day; one time
to wake you, another to check
your sleep. You reside, breathe

in this moment time has no word
for; neither past, nor future,
I miss, I wish do not trickle
from your silent tongue.

Ephemera

Curios

Welcome to the Museum of Marvels!
Come in from the mizzle,
into the making of moonlight.
where the masqued mummer spins

a frozen pirouette.
Mog into the annex, note
the kitschy painting of the maroon
bowl mud sliding its rim with blue mussels

and sweet mazzards.
Like the muezzin calling the faithful
to prayer, the mockingbird medlies
a mythical tune from the maze

of a musty annex. Meditate
upon the diorama exhibit
of a taxidermal muskox,
museful in its wide

meanderings of muskeg.
Come! Muddle through a mystic's
archive of stuffed mallards, of mammoth
tusk. Curate your mango-sweet
curiosity.

Second-Hand

Musty, like your
grandmother's closet
long unopened.

Mirrored doors slide
and rattle, accelerate
to an open road

of polyester, wool,
leather, and spandex;
immaterial, for the right

price. Strappy sandals,
Chanel clutch, mink stole,
bejeweled Maple leaf brooch.

From estate sale
to consignment shop,
the shuffle of goods,

of paisley scarves,
knitted sweaters, silky
pantsuits cruise the free-

way between departure
and destination. Pick
your poison; fill a bag.

Assemblage

Garish in color and scope, I nest
my creating space with ephemera,
both foraged and thieved. Women

and *corvidae* take flight
from their stretched canvas
perch either in spirit or wing.

Gathered in empty candle-
holders, dusty stones (green
opal, orange calcite, tree agate)

charge by moonlight, blush
pale luminosity in wan
afternoon shine. Feather

of a grey jay, blue luster
radiates twinkle light glint.
Mugs thieved from Tim Hortons

house beads (Czech, lampwork,
crackle, evil eye). Tumbled drift-
wood, lake smooth, dry. Tiny

carved owls wonder wide-eyed
from high shelves, ponder
the branch they've never

known, the wings they've
never tested, wedged among
stacks of origami-paged books.

Postage Due

Dear Raven Lady. Dear M/V *Taku*, Marine Ferry Space Traveler of the Outer Coast Scrapped on the Shore of Alang, India. Dear Levenger of Smooth Ink Pen and Welcoming Paper. Dear Friend Cutting Lime and Lemon Slices for Gin and Tonics. Dear Giddy Laughter. Dear Artist Sitting at the Table Forming Wings from Polymer Clay; Brush Stroking Verdi Gris, Polyester Blue Highlights. Dear Dad Needing a McCulloch Gas Line and Filter from Ebay. Dear Chicken Breast and Steamed Broccoli. Dear Holding Out for Gale and Darkness. Dear Fumes of June. Dear Kluane. Dear Daughter of Eggplant Hair and Grit. Dear Pumpkin Spice Friend Dropping F-Bombs at Every Meeting. Fuck. And F u c k Again. Dear Cyclical Opening to Page One Each and Every Day: Outage, Silence, Dreams Gone South; Repeat. Dear Crack of Book Spine to Read-Agains and First Reads: *To Kill a Mockingbird, Songs of a Wild Yak*. Dear Tangerine Moon and Late-Night Squall. Dear Energy. Dear Honey Crisp Apple Wobbling Across the Counter. Dear Stillness and Crying Gulls. Dear Moving Forward. Dear Cards that Read of Someday Again Maybe Good Fortune. Dear Telepathy, Send Him a Message - I Am Ready.

Letters unwritten;
words form, rattle in standstill
before the waking.

Clutter

We serve our endless day
in the child's bedroom,
raking nameless clutter

from her reading nook.
A rainbow of rubble
balloons across the floor:

gum wrappers, mismatched
baby doll shoes, Pokémon
cards (standard playground

trading fare), books read
in triplicate, dirty socks left
behind by one holiday cousin,

or another. The *goddamnit*
surprise of a Lego under a bare
foot, hunk of lava, crumbled star-

fish under the other. Like Houdini's
sleight of hand, I fill trash bags
on the sly, convince her to rehome

the oversized stuffed dog, Minnie
Mouse. Tonight, she slumbers,
wrapped in orderly dreams.

Le Creuset

The Earth spins west
to east. A waxed
patchouli moon,
carves a sucker hole
through nimbostratus.

Is this the dawn
of leaf-dropping
rains, williwaw
of a season's
deviation?

My mother-in-law
stands at the sink
in my kitchen.
At 72, her shoulders
arc crescent;

they are warm
under the curve
of my palm.
She marvels
at the Caribbean

blue of my new
frying pan,
too heavy to hang
from the pot rack.

Her hands, timeworn,
furrowed like the thoughts
carried on her brow, they hew
the cloud cover of suds,
scour clockwise.

Used Goods

Welcome to the online garage sale,
the second-hand shop of your mind
where the fertile eggs of white elephant

gifts abound. Welcome to the place
you can find the treasures you never
knew you needed: the 1970's bathtub

Jesus for the yard, Barbie Doll's friend
to cure her loneliness on the shelf,
the flaming tiki goods for patio

parties. You, too, can live the reclaimed
life of a retired queen, a repurposed
existence adorned with rhinestone bling,

the shuffle hush of non-recyclable grocery
store bags filled with the turquoise sky
of potential, filled with your salvation.

Dutch Fry Baby

We sit at the island
in my turquoise kitchen
our hands warmed
by hot coffee, by mugs
of stoneware pottery.

When I was a child,
you warmed my hands
in the hold of your hands,
or in the pocket
of a Woolrich jacket.

Today's mug up is rooted
in warmth and bribery.
The driveway too slick
to safely maneuver
with shovel is plowed

by you. In turn, the winds
of Ceylon cinnamon blow.
The egg and baked apple,
the butter, flour and brown
sugar counter your bluster.

Like you, this morning
is brisk.

Men Who Serve You Coffee

-For Karen

Steamy, like men who wake
before the bawdy gaze of day
to capture water before boil,
flood the press, clatter around

your kitchen barefooted, beaned:
French Roast, Yukon Chaga,
simple Folgers; of little matter,
but served in bed. Swarthy

like *picea mariana*, heady boreal,
you walk among the seed and layers
of rafters, skiers, smooth talkers,
loggers. Coffee, a story, a heart

lost to a longshoreman, chance
encounters with international
politicos who confirm your beauty,
offer refugee status should you

one day cross that border
between *what is* and *could be*.
To the plangency of beat-skipping
bar tunes, two-stepping wildly

with lanky fathers, sons, your
own wild spirit cupped in the nest
of your palm, wrapping your hands
around a hot mug in the morning.

Copy of a Copy

With money, boredom,
you can do anything.
You can stroll the Champs-
Élysées singing the old

hits, "The Way We Were,"
in your head, wade through
pooled cherry blossom drift,
walk your Coton de Tuléar

puppy on gem-encrusted
leash, its clone ghost
Samantha nipping
at your heels.

Honey Sound

All swing & sway
hips & flesh
mauve lamé

sun-bounce sheer
sleek rhinestones
plastic dinosaur

women & children
marigold wall boys
hipping hula hoops

naked baby butt
feral earrings bouncy
RV blinged-out

mosaic of afghan
breeze-caught curtain
lion mural, record shop

soul-sinewed Kali
loose bun hair
spin & dizzy

Lessons Learned from Scandia Noir

Live only in this moment, the past is dead –
not so different from the body washed up on shore.
You can survive on dill pickles, rye bread,
frozen pizza, organic espresso from El Salvador.

Forgo the greeting, answer calls with your name.
All that personal angst, depression, anxiety, bury
between the frozen, clouded panes of a window frame.
Ignore the boss, his endless points teeter over weary,

and if you forget to carry your gun into a precarious setting
you have your wits about you, the hopeful politeness
of humanity, the living without bothersome regretting,
you can still neutralize a threat, render them lifeless.

And it is ever snowing. And in the case of a golden
brief glow of summer, don't fret. Winter is beholden.

All Things Gray

Silvered highlights. Ashen clouds rendering
Maxfield Parrish sucker holes. Veined

greywacke mapping imaginary river systems.
I want to go there. Oysters on the half shell,

Guinness chasers. Ashy remains of a midwinter
bonfire, likewise the smoky start of a woodstove

on frigid winter mornings, its signature heather
writing against an iron sky. Hair salted and peppered

with age and wisdom, dappled with *I don't care*
and *Let's do it*.

Bohemian

If on days my husband works late
and our daughter twirls in silks anchored
to high ceilings, and I can sneak

away from the paper bear of work
at a bell's release, I walk home
and light the stinky candles:

Moonbeams on Pumpkin, Salted Caramel.
I stretch my uphill-weary legs across
the leather ottoman to sunbathe in diluted

autumn rays. And if on days I bask
in an early return home, supper simmering
on a back burner, and my drunk neighbor

cranks Fleetwood Mac on his tinny stereo,
I'll dance wildly, spin, pretend that my voice
is Stevie's:

> *Lightning strikes maybe once,*
> *maybe twice. Oh, and it lights up the night.*
> *And you see you're a gypsy.*

Lyrics from "Gypsy" written by Stevie Nicks, 1979.

Cataclysm

Crop

In his days of forget-me-not
wild iris softball trips

he was a shooting star of bat,
chocolate lily drink & story.

From Dustball to Mudball,
I'd stretch my columbine

ears to hear the details
giggled over by dogwood men,

until one by one they bluebelled
into self-proclaimed beer-

league retirement. Lupine,
blue poppy, like fireweed

we burn summer bright,
flashy, charismatic,

until we settle
into seed & soil.

Da Eye Wifey / Woods Number 1

Title borrowed from the band Shooglenifty.

Emerge from the fog road
squint-eyed
to belly flopping waves
jumping from one small sea-
sick ferry to another
saltwater & cod tongues
summer grasses & violet lupine.
Northern Blues swarm
the sunlit forest.
Awakened, we ramble;
Trans-Canada Highway
from west to east
and back again.
Mile 0,
I'd follow you forever.
Chime of cymbal,
song's end.

Winning

Do you remember
that casino in Halifax?
We carried a gallon Ziploc
of loose change —
loonies, toonies —
laundry money
for the road.

Grip lost, coins deluged
across camouflaged
carpet in dim light.
Crawling, we giggled,
scooped, shoveled,
took off before
kicked out.

You were always
my *cha-ching*
in the change drop;
my big win
payout, triple
jackpot,
flashing
light.

Safe Harbor

Do you remember when storm
Was synonymous with loving?
An offshore gale pole vaulting
Across the island to rattle
Our window, you'd kiss the

Nape of my neck, dimpled shoulder,
Feathered scintillation of one
Thousand blue-winged butterflies,
Flitting restless in the sunlit portal
Of the forest. And later, tangled

In sheets, we'd drowse. My fingertips
Tracing lazy mandalas on your back,
My thoughts drift, rest upon stillness
In the pin-cushioned eye of memory,
The echo of the storm.

Cèilidh for Angus

To a canticle of wind
and juncos, squalls trip
across a sullen ocean
an errant curtain hop-
scotches across the sill
of an open window.

I want no somber dirge,
no plodding funeral song.
Instead, the screaming
banshee of a wicked fiddler,
of more hair than voice,
of ear and aura, of other-

worldly and techno fusion.
Now, the wave of dancers crests
and rolls, plummets, falls head-
long into a sea of bow
and string. After, the swallow
of kitchen party Jamison,
the echo of last notes step
dance among embers.

With a lone seal, you swim,
cross this sound
into another.

Island of Lost

Here, husbands
disappear. They fall
over gunwales, sink
into murky tea-leaf
sea. Eyes to cedar
bough-quilted
sky, they walk
into the forest

lose track
of their bread-
crumb trail.
Sometimes,
they lose
their breath.
Here, on the island
of lost husbands

wives wait,
their children
scamper rocky
shore, overturn
rocks for hermit
crabs, bullheads,
footprints formed,
erased by tide.

Too soon

you
disappear

into the mountain
range of my mind
to wander summit

and rift. The lake
of three guardsmen
protects my frozen heart.

In spring, I'll give chase,
look for you in the place
the gulls nest.

The Geography of Grief

It's a bit like a cauliflower, really,
no bend, all hardened parts, semi-

hardened parts, snap. It's a bit
like a cauliflower, really, sitting

sedentary on the equators of a midnight
dark hallway, the one you stumble

through from bed to bathroom in search
of Kleenex. It's a bit like a cauliflower,

really, uncooked, raw reminders
of the continent of loss, of loss, of loss.

Cut

Your voice in my ear,
I move from one task to another:

Set the morning alarm,
wake our daughter, wrap my mind

around another day without you.
I'll grade the papers as if breathing,

record numbers, teach stories that read
like the veins in my wrist. There are many

ways to slice an onion, sad tale, memory
the sharpest blade among the knives.

Status Update

Lost in memory updates:
6, 4, 2 years ago. A silly meme
about stars stealing my hair,

blaming the celestial
for bad behavior,
smart ass banter

with my missing man,
our daughter outgrowing
picture books for chapters.

I'd like to check-in
at 47 below, deactivate,
sleep.

Signs

Did I miss
the mile markers?
The signs? Dead
lilac bush in spring,

raspberry canes
stripped of verdancy,
their fat digit fruits
a memory from August

past. Moss-tangled flower
beds, the wild Yukon rose
you gifted me, grown amok.
I'd give all the dandelions

pushing through hard ground,
coiled fiddleheads, the first
blush of rhododendron bloom,
for one more autumn with you.

Shroud

-After Bob Kaufman's, "I Have Folded My Sorrows"

I fold my sorrows
in the dim shadow

of underbrush
where it is damp,

dank, quiet.
The day's light

is slow to reach
this shade, origin

of cane, trunk,
stem. The scrim

of the underbelly,
leaf-litter, weed-

tangle, a gathering
of scree, this

is where I crawl.

Unaccounted For

This separation,
this death
did us part,
splitting of sheet,

spring break-up
of far northern rivers:
Yukon, Tanana,
Kuskokwim.

This season
of potholes
and dog shit.
A waking bear,

my love sports
a phantom limb,
an unplanned
amputation.

Little Salmon Lake

In my half-dream,
the black bear follows
under thread strung
leaves in opal apple
hues — not quite flame,
but golden — circling
the roots of poplar,
white birch, anchored
in hoarfrost.

And in this half-dream,
I trail you into the forest
peppered by leaf fall,
crusted and rimed,
our laughter as warm
as the promised soup pot
after a cold trek to a cabin
we did not acquire
its windows eyeing

the lake. Anguish
is tangible; the pocked
skin of a mandarin.
At the sun's tumble,
the world flares
orange — our old joy
the fruit inside —
as daylight roots
into dusk.

Perennial

Enraged, the land wildfires (lightning match sparks kindle). The lines shift, adjust like a kelp-tossed shore by a tide whose water is not gifted for battle. Suppression waxes / wanes while crew and beast meander burnout, their forms mere shadows in the charcoaled smoke. Hazed / dazed, the sun is a pinhole viewed through a sepia filter; blood orange rimmed crimson, a sleepless eye. I hear fireweed is the first returner / responder to a stand of black spruce crisped / aged to lustrous toothpicks for years after a fiery event. Pale standing wood bears luminous signature, runes of warning / evacuation, calamitous loss. Grounded in a house of time, rooted in both memory / future, fireweed unfolds her foliate arms in ravaged / displaced forest, coaxed by stellar light / instinct. Hers is a ground swelling tease, a verdant display of spring sprout (green lush leaf), undulating arms beckoning breeze. As she lays hands on ravaged wood, her summer frenzy shimmies into amaranthine glow, speaking in tongues efflorescence. Nectar beguiles both bee / hummer in a short, splendid upsurge of growth / violaceous bloom. Casting seed, she dances like a groupie to Neil Young's "Harvest Moon," before blazing mottled tiger yam, drooping under fall rains / freezing temperatures.

Head to ground, she weeps
in rains not knowing words
of loss, grief, return.

Astral

96% of the universe

consists of the dark
and unknown

Dabble too long
in the night
and your eyes
sharpen

Read text
by shape
shadow
and star

Wander
in aimless
flight
Pursue

this glimmer
and sheen
into the blue
dark of morning

Birth of a Black Hole

Star,
your birth,
bastardly backward
as it may be,
beckons bright
and bigger

than baggage
and bankruptcy.
Bayonet
the Bajeezus
out of blazoned
blessings.

Backhand
the blankness
of bayberry
bulbs, bawdy
beadwork,
bustling sky.

Moonset

Grapefruit moon
umbrellas morning sky,
accords me a sly wink

before tucking in
behind Camel Back.
I swear she anchors

a towline to night,
rope climbs her way
to *super* and *blue*

and the fiery show-
stopper of a lunar
eclipse. She slides

into rest leaving only
the glow of sodium
lights in the harbor.

Harvest Moon Aubade

I woke this morning
before the break of dawn
certain to catch a glimpse
of the bright moon's path,
however fleeting in its long
night's run. As the way
of a rainforest, a drapery
of clouds obscured the sky's
window. Rooibos in hand,
I settle to watch the time
lapse of crater sky casting
light upon another day.
I ponder the soggy garden,
the onions that need pulling,
the peas and their picking.
I ponder the days once
called summer.

Charged Particles

Nothing but north wind,
black coffee night sky patterned
by quartz chipped stars. Fortified

by red wine, chunked chocolate
our pre-ski *apéritif* warmed the blood.
Wrapped in Arctic gear, we crossed

and looped the ice fast lagoon glissading
parallel to the Chukchi Sea. Shuffle
and glide of cross-country skis sound-

tracked by laughter at our dogs, unwilling
skijorers; laughter at the brittle hollow
burst of thirty below, of home far

from home, that midnight crack
of loneliness shelved and distant.

Stjerne

the word for star
in Danish & Norwegian.
My girl cups this heritage

like a lapis lazuli palmstone;
veins of cosmic clutter
pattern her worldview.

Archaic pantheons,
invented deities visit her
from the smooth-printed page:

Saint Luna of the cobalt sky;
Saint Cedar of the windswept
forest, of family and forage;

Saint Constellation
of the stories toe-tipping
their way into dreams.

Beyond Neptune

Land and sea kindle outside
the glass pane window, full moon
sweeps in her pregnant form, tugs

at the tide, casts far-reaching umbra
of the alder tree's branch, the rusted bird-
house, the neighbor's planked fence,

against the weather-worn southern wall
of the house. Inside, the aberration
of hum, the vibrational

glow of the Milky Way projects, spins
against the ceiling, the fixed North Star
blanketed in star dust, glow in the dark

plastic constellations orbit the space
from their fixed positions. In the corner,
a galaxy hoodie drapes over a chair.

The daughter and her cat sleep soundly,
stellar storms and storylines cross valleys,
summit peaks in aimless dreams, write

horoscopes in the comet's tail of slumber.
Here in the quiet hush, a syzygy
of moon, terra, and child.

Juncture

To the Bare Salmonberry Branch in Winter Cold

-After James Wright's "To the Saguaro Cactus Tree in the Desert Rain"

I'm not certain how tiny juncos
twitter and flit through your maze
of stalks.

I have tried to extricate myself from sharp-thorned
memory, that seems

tangled and impossible at night.
I wish to be the somber shadow
of raven, I wish I were
the slink of river otter
and the perched patience of eagle.
I have no idea how you summon
your spring greens,
blush of June bloom.
I shiver in winter near the sea,
the often rain,
so, I quit.

Teach me to hope again.

Pushing Forward

I am first-cut lawn sporting horsetails –
seasoned green, winter worn along the margins
of the yard.

Newly-planted pansies spilled on the porch –
granulated potting soil, Styrofoam dry,
crumbled,

encircling sunny viola faces, lemon and twilight.
I am the boulder in the rock wall, cracked
in stillness, halved,

dropped in the steep slope of the driveway.
But I am not the Anna's hummingbird, delicate
yet deliberate it its search for sugar water,

in its flutter, together in its iridescence,
purpose. Sharp in whir and border,
I am not this.

Diminishing Wind

Drunk *corvidae*
shake the branches
of the mountain
ash: teeter, stretch,
devour fermented

fruit. Drunk in this
day's ascending light,
the silhouette
of a teetering raven
balances

in a nearby alder.
This is how you
create the wind;
this is how you
ride it.

Da Vinci's *A Bear Walking*

An eerie likeness
between a bear's paw
and a human's hand.

We don't realize this
until the bear is skinned,
splayed on a blue tarp,

cracked open for viewing.
Hands hold the power
to grab, fend, and cuff;

protect the young, sustain.
Our hands can dart, miss
the mark, dispatch

the wild beast roaming
the dark woods, traveling
its enduring trails.

Heartwood

Sun glazing my back
I flex my arms
above my head.

My shape shifts
into a dark alder,
umbra against

a warming ground.
With the wind
I sway and creak

remembering
the language of trees
shared by my logger

father: crown, trunk
root. Raven hovers
on a high branch

cocks his dodgy
one-eyed look, peering
for sweet treats tucked

in the tight buds
of my hands. Leaf,
needle, cone, flower.

Of Alderaan

"I want it reported that I drowned in moonlight,
strangled by my own bra." - Carrie Fisher

I don't know if Princess
Leia covets superhero
status, if over-the-ear

cinnamon buns convey
signature style. When
the neighborhood boys,

my brothers and I played
Star Wars along boulder-
piled coastline and forested

paths, I was Leia — not sidekick
metal-bikini Leia, but hero
Leia, swooping in for rescues,

saves, and smart decisions.
I was Leia of the Star Chamber
and the Star Chamber was mine.

Sometimes

I'll park in a driveway
that's not mine, take
in the view as if it were:
aged tugboat, pretty penny
waterfront homes, over-
priced auditorium echoing
its own silence —

I contemplate a fresh color
for a front door I'll not open:
orange moon, or teal. Starry
lobelia, red geraniums shoot
from a green moss basket, hanging
from a rusted, empty hook —

in the greenhouse that is not mine
the leafy vine hosting cherry tomatoes
pushes skyward, wraps around the center
beam, the border between *I have*
and *I dream.*

Minus Tide

Beneath the full moon
of a flashlight's beam:
starfish hatchery.

Tiny five-armed stars
bed among sea grass,
the rocking cradle

of tidal current.
The expanse of beach
mirrors the black sky

and raingear-garbed,
we marvel at low tide
creatures, the moment,
of being alive.

Tsunami

Only in myth
can a little boy swallow the sea.
Mirth measured by slow inhale,
the unveiling of an ocean's floor.
Come in.

Have a seat at the epicenter,
an empty table of wonder.
Here, a skipping stone trail
of orange sea stars, flip of a coin
rockfish flopping among rivulets

of water seeping from under
the cloth, masking the heave
and split of solid legs. Before
the aftershock, the first motion,
the seiche.

A screaming surge crests,
tumbles into a trough.
Without warning, the crack
and splinter of wood, disappearance
into a wall of water,
the stillness.

Prayer for the Wildness

For the step off the trail
into the boreal sponge,
the muskeg of your mind
where the dead mingle

with your memory,
like your boot trapped
in the bog. Prayer
for the squat shore pine,

a contortionist eking
out a living in sodden space,
its resin sealing unspoken
words on your tongue.

The Ungulate's Jaw

In the summer of her life
she'd rest and forage.

Her lips and rough tongue
gathered horsetail, red elder-

berry, paper birch, willow.
She'd bed down in a grass-flattened

patch, mandala-round, surrounded
by low bushes, deciduous greens

cracking their vellum leaves
in the afternoon warmth and wind.

In the fall, the cow, a road-kill
casualty, fed six families in need.

A bone collector from Talkeetna
carried home her jawbone, bleached

crescent moon dry and white
by the hyperborean sun. She took

it home, drilled tiny holes into the smooth
sled runner below its molars.

From each, she tied a string of glass beads,
of whispering bells. The moose cow will sing

again, of summer greens and twigs, sing
again, from an ocean-view window.

Haines Highway

-after Ted Kooser

The highway winds
like a slow clock along
the Chilkat River, dandelion

seeds waft to the empyrean.
This, the second hand of Alaska.
Riding the curves, you miss him

at the wheel, your eyes darting
upward, catching morning
light flounce its patch-

worked skirt among peaks
whose names are known
only by locals. Just before

the border crossing, a road-
side lake. A trumpeter swan,
or two, claim residence.

Sapsuckers hammer
burrows into snags, flit
and flutter from the forest

to their young. You feel
like that, mother your child
from afar, hover between

the world of foliage, and a bare-
wood nest. You feel like sliding
into the shoulder, setting

the emergency brake. You
feel like walking into the canopy,
into the mountain's lantern.

To the Cabin Named Mary Jane

Carry with you the stones, the worn papered journal. Set lined paper and pen aside. Instead of one linear page after another, write your thoughts on the cloud-dappled sky with cherry-blossomed branch: floral ink, sharpened wood utensil. Baby red-breasted sapsuckers will visit you on the front porch, cry for words, peer inside the open chamber of your heart. They cock their tiny heads at the scrape of a chair, the tinny whine of a chime. Who could apperceive their inquisitiveness, their stretched-neck feline curiosity? We all crane our necks for the whimsical, the weird, the unknown: Louis Armstrong's "What a Wonderful World" buttering rooftops on a gusty summer night, slant spotlight crazy quilting wild iris, babbled exchange of aurora and wildfire at Windy Arm. Sweet husband, you emerged from a land of strawberries and cream, a baby weaned on oatmeal, Malt-O Meal, whole milk. You were born for the far away, the crinkle-eyed squint for green flash before the dark. I will know you again, the flick of your wrist, your calloused fingertips pushing flecks of gold into the safety of seam, the separation of precious from ordinary. Gather this glimmer in tiny vials to net sun sheen from a windowsill. I want to drink every last drop, Goldschläger gone rogue with Yukon wild, mineral marveled by your warm touch. It has never mixed easily with the earth, this halcyon, this summer of present tense.

Oh, sweet cabin of
stout walls, spirit: writing can
save your goddamn life.

Quartz

My fingertips read
this chunk of amethyst.
From its story spills
a time-capsuled
house, a calendar
page from 1995:
bottles, critters
in the basement,
tea leaves, signs
of mice.

Outside, the moose
cow beds down,
flattens tall grasses
in lavender dusk.

The stone's jagged peaks
sporting alpenglow
red dive into kamikaze
free falls, the handwritten
script of what remains.

Epilogue

Write

On my final breath
let me write a death poem
to daughter and stars:
Alchemy of days, of road,
of returning to the earth.

Kersten Christianson is the author of *Something Yet to Be Named* (Kelsay Books, 2017) and *What Caught Raven's Eye* (Petroglyph Press, 2018). Her poetry has published in *Camas Magazine, San Pedro River Review, The Bangor Literary Journal, Whiskey Island, The Northern Review,* and elsewhere. She's the recipient of a writer's residency at Alderworks Alaska Writers & Artists Retreat. She is the poetry editor of *Alaska Women Speak*. Kersten holds an MFA in Creative Writing and the Literary Arts from the University of Alaska Anchorage. By career, she is a secondary English teacher. She lives by the tides in Sitka, Alaska, where she raises her daughter, tracks the moon, walks among ravens, and makes a dash across the border to the Yukon any chance she's given.

Inspired by life and layers, artist Cara Jane Murray creates with the eye of a multidisciplinary artist and muralist. Cara's spirited work explores the imprints of strife and jubilation. Limitless in medium, the strength of her art is rooted in its ability to evoke the inspired human spirit in all of its blunders and triumphs. Her positive, uplifting style serves to remind us that we are both great and small in this wild world.

Born and raised in Southeast Alaska, Cara's style illustrates an extensive graphic design background combined with a love for contemporary folk art and the expansiveness of Alaska. Both maker and mother, she resolves to stay open, clear and connected to a sense of place while remaining fluid in her spiritual experience.

Cara believes art will continue to serve as the most honest and expansive form of communication that can ever be shared and this is how she gives, heals, rallies courage, loves and illuminates her heart.

Sheila-Na-Gig Editions

CPSIA information can be obtained
at www.ICGtesting.com
Printed in the USA
LVHW052146170920
666329LV00012B/427